Ambrosia

Love Poems

by

Mark D. Bennion

Finishing Line Press
Georgetown, Kentucky

Ambrosia

Love Poems

Copyright © 2024 by Mark D. Bennion
ISBN 979-8-88838-528-9 First Edition
All rights reserved under International and Pan-American Copyright Conventions. No part of this book may be reproduced in any manner whatsoever without written permission from the publisher, except in the case of brief quotations embodied in critical articles and reviews.

ACKNOWLEDGMENTS

Versions of these poems have appeared in the following publications. I appreciate the editors for their willingness to take a chance on these poems.

Compass Rose Literary Journal, "Liminal Space"
Furrow, "Descent"
Impostor: A Poetry Journal, "Breezeway"
The Good Men Project, "Not Quite the River of Tears"
Radix, "What I've Thought and What Is"
Shemom, "Pregnancy"
Windhover. "Holding Your Hand in Bed" & "Sacrament"

"Tree of Life" was published in *Psalm & Selah: a poetic journey through the Book of Mormon* (Bentley Enterprises, 2009).

"Holding Your Hand in Bed," "Pregnancy," and "Sacrament" all appeared in the collection *Beneath the Falls: poems* (Resource Publications, 2021).

A book of this nature arrives slowly over time, perception, experience, and reflection. My gratitude goes to colleagues, friends, and family members who have shaped these poems into better, clearer versions. Special thanks, too, to Dr. Lynita Newswander and her students—Danielle Davenport, Ethan Hunt, Jack Jerman, Kaden Walker, and Rachel Welker—for providing excellent feedback and editorial assistance.

Of course, the lion's share of my appreciation goes to Kristine for her unending devotion, boundless candor, and abundant love. She is my muse and always will be.

Publisher: Leah Huete de Maines
Editor: Christen Kincaid
Cover Art: Mark D. Bennion
Author Photo: James Allen
Cover Design: Elizabeth Maines McCleavy

Order online: www.finishinglinepress.com
also available on amazon.com

Author inquiries and mail orders:
Finishing Line Press
PO Box 1626
Georgetown, Kentucky 40324
USA

Contents

I

Backstory 2
Valentine's Day 2000 3
Going to the Sun 4
Charley Horse 5
Sijo for Annae 7
One 8
Birth 9
Pregnancy 10

II

Breezeway 12
Rafting 13
Thursday 14
Ode to Montana 15
Not Quite the River of Tears 17
Sacrament 18
Liminal Space 19
Descent 20

III

Ambrosia 24
She Calls Me by My First Name 25
Tree of Life 26
Every Kind of Twin 28
Choice 29
What I've Thought and What Is 30
44 31
Post-Anniversary Thoughts 33
Holding Your Hand in Bed 34

For Kristine—Reformer, Dreamer, Wonder
(July 20, 2000)

I

Backstory

We met in the rapture of an '80s dance,
an excuse to exorcise the inner minions
of whatever baggage we carried at the end
of 1999, our two lives no more held together

than nails and sawdust. Sweat and smolder
streaming onto my shirt, your folded arms
dismissive of lavender streamers
and tepid hot chocolate. Your eyebrows

resolute, your ears attuned to hours
of conversation and mouth yearning
for the purity of water. We felt distanced
in that exchange until that exchange

wrapped its carpet and music around us
on Valentine's Day two months later,
setting free the failures and nuances
of past relationships, lungs filling

with the candor of winter air
and the scent of new letters. Our strolls
at night pried something loose
from the ribcage, a kind of Thurberian

penchant for cartoons, a bit of Wildese
spilling out in your questions, my repartee.
No scrapbook or Nikon to capture
that initial incident and rising action.

Just several moments of arm locking,
restaurant hopping, testimony bearing
to whisk us out of the platonic cave.
Shadows clung like wrinkles to our clothing.

The words You and I morphed into heart
shapes, rippled like echoes in a museum
or canyon. Our hands fastened, bolted
to each other, secure as a locked door or sight.

Valentine's Day 2000

The screams of Y2K turn to nostalgia.
The Clintons are taking their final months
of pseudo victory laps. In Missoula,

a young woman traces the last four years
of her life like a child
who memorizes the colors of horizons.

Heart-shaped post-it notes
greet her beloved before he can find
keys to the door, any door.

He boils water for pasta and carrots.
She looks to finish any moment
with song.

They slide open the window of the past
and dab toward the watercolor
of the future—hands of children
arising out of clay and ash.

Going to the Sun

We stop outside my grandmother's apartment,
taking one last photo before we fuse
the left ventricles of our hearts together
for the rest of here and now and forever,

Soon we will rest in the celestial
room of the Salt Lake Temple, celebrate
woodwork and engravings by 19th century
craftsmen, clutch one another's hands

as if they hold the secrets of each pioneer,
each convert, each ancestor praying
and weeping for us to be here.
We are no longer from Whitefish and Ephraim,

no longer soccer star and tennis champ,
no more two travelers on separate continents
packing up souvenirs to keep on lone,
uneven shelves. We are a pink dress

and navy suit wrapped in an embrace
to pivot time. We are the valley to catch
rain and sun, tornado and breeze.
We are mountain rising out of lava

and streams, forging our way
with granite, pine, and dust. We hop
into the car, head to the House of the Lord,
riding from the earth toward the sun,

the light and heat slowly swirling,
shaping our new sanctuary,
our life beginning to beam and burn
in the corona of blessing and affliction,

a life we choose to give to the other
before scanning witnesses, beneath topaz
in crystals, beside loved ones who push
and pray for us in this ray of ascension.

Charley Horse

You awaken at 3:00 a.m.
gripping
at the mound of pain

secluded inside your calf
gnawing
on your harp-string tendons

for those seconds
lasting
longer than five dreams,

and all I can think of
barely
is the moment

you forgot the words
to "The Star Spangled Banner"
at the state high school wrestling tournament,

and the time you craved
popcorn
and pickles and pancakes,

you rattled on about
cramps
how they'd leave you

for at least three days or as long as
your fling
with that bodybuilder

I nicknamed Stretch. You sit up,
try
to touch those eggshell

toenails, ask me to rub the burning
flesh
as if my hands were ice. I

attempt to scatter that
scorching
into retreat, to caress

so long that neither of
us
will know whose muscles

ached. You lie
down
brushing aside the night's

phantoms, your arms
release
the mountain of covers.

I hear your deep breath
whirling
like a breeze after the rain

and your calf
glistens
like glass pulled from the fire.

Sijo for Annae

When we married, I tried to teach you the Korean alphabet,
sounding out consonants quickly, skipping over the vowels.
You made kimchi, japchae, fire meat, and seaweed soup instead.

One

I envision you, as I envision us
in a moment more canonized, more honestly
pure, that we are *nuclear mysticism*,
a brush with a suspended hand or rose:
painters, clinical about sky, detailing
chiaroscuro in New York and Port Lligat;
the stance of Gala and Dalí
winds us through the palette of night—
from the eclipsing violet to the olive tan—
guides us into the morning air.
By dawn, we sing.

Birth
After Linda Pastan

More anticipated
than the first day of school
or opening night
it calls you to rearrange
the furniture, even in the laundry room.

More feared than stolen wallet,
car rollover, or dissertation defense,
it becomes more insatiable
with each passing month
and every sociable question.

At seven months, you lumber
down the road
and in the elevator.
Those you don't know
are afraid to ask anything.

How cumbersome
to cut your toenails,
to lengthen each breath.
Before, you didn't notice
your ankles or knees.

The neck
grows ruddier with each step.
You are ready to sleep
standing up.
And if the pain leads you
to ask the doctor one final question,
wait for the baby to answer it.

Pregnancy

For thirty-two months out of the past
nine years the squirm of joint
and muscle, elbow and kick have swung

beneath your ribs, caused you to pause
some mornings at the base of stairs.
In the welling up of your belly,

such twisting legs and aching flesh,
such wispy, scarecrow knuckles
have been enough to drive you into afternoons

of slumber. Not one month, or one week,
has been less important than the others
as swelling nerves continue to stiffen

your back and sharpen your ears
for the nights of cat-naps to follow.
Again, you ready as the interior world

winds up its knock, when you'll offer
your body to its own deep rivers
and treacherous streams, to those slippery,

trilling words: *bear down, push,
one more time*; this journey is ineluctable.
Yet, even now you understand

how these first few months begin
to pull you outside of yourself
while the rest of us look on, in stupor

and wonder, waiting for the fire and aura
of the flexible crown, the streaked body,
the colored cord, the life.

II

Breezeway

Some days I stood there waiting,
watching rain pelt the ground
or snow drift like feathers.

And sometimes I'd linger
between the Smith Annex
and the classrooms
teeming with students, recalling
their compliments and questions,
wondering when you'd come
to pick me up.

The wind tunneled through me
when a colleague opened the door.
My mind yearned for the verve
of pre-dinner conversation
and the ritual of reading to each other.
The bedtime stories tucked
me in, especially when you told them.

Before long, each child entered
the hallway of your belly
always connecting the threads
of desire, sometimes coming
between the hungers of the heart.

Your voice, then as now,
sweet as powdered sugar,
candid as salt. Both flavors
landing nightly on my lips.
I can still taste the contrasts

when I find any arch
connecting two places,
and I wait for your words
and our children's laughter
to rise like the April sun
after a long winter.

Rafting

We lean back in our life jackets
and sunglasses, next to other couples
from St. Louis and South Dakota, while
the air teases us in a back and forth
of breeze and heat. We are strangers
who speak easily of our children
and professions, of dreams
that glide like morning light
fording through the trees. We are so close
to euphoria and inner stillness
at the surge of rapids, hollering
at the water's temperature, wondering
how the oar becomes part of the hand,
telling the others, as if we're old friends,
we're celebrating 11 years of marriage.
We understand a little of the sharper turns,
those leading to vistas of boulder and pine
taller than buildings, and the whitewater
quickens and terrifies, leaves us
glazed in beads of river and sweat.

And before we can raise a glass
to the entire group and send them on
to other sites, we're changing back
into our regular clothes, to thoughts
of washing the car and cleaning the house.
Out of the water we barely know
how to move our tongues or say goodbye.
We're just an old married couple now,
turning the car toward the future and home,
back to the chalk talk of weekly schedules
and garbage pickup, the sheen of the Snake
River fading, trying to remember the names
of each person, but instead we speak of eating
Thai food for lunch. We know it's bound to come,
that moment when we return to whose turn
it is to sweep the kitchen floor
and clean out the garage.

Thursday

You share with me:
All good things
happen on Thursday. You say it
early in the morning
when the bird chatter sparkles
and sometimes you whisper it
when the house is dark.

I nod knowingly,
somehow reborn with assurance
that an old friend
might reach out over email
or an authentic Italian restaurant
will soon grace our high desert town.

I hear your voice long after
I've gone to work. The cadence
like water rolling over stones,
like awe that purls
before a Thanksgiving feast.

Ode to Montana

O infinite sky mirroring plains and blessings,
O land of cottonwoods, western red cedars,
wide swaths of Rocky Mountain and creeping junipers,
stately solitude, corners dusty and folded

like forgotten maps, you were the pen and muse
of Wallace Stegner and Ivan Doig, Patricia Goedicke
and Richard Hugo, their words bringing
others out of urban nests. You contain

the breath of the midnight driver, the force
for the reasonable and prudent highwayman
outside Dillon or Glendive. You are the lone soldier
or last survivor from the Battle of Little Bighorn

and the cattle rancher driving his team beyond
the grip of Colstrip. Nearly 100 years
after statehood, you raised my sweetheart
from an almost 12-year-old, rollicking adolescent

to a nails and hammer teenager, preparing her
for a Granite Peak journey to adulthood.
In her fortieth year, she knows more
than any drug store psychology text

could ever tell her
that Big Sky is larger than forest fires
and Greek myths, that the land
still pries open unknown hives and enchantment.

I see her skiing her way through winter,
poles locked in her fingertips; she shuttles
down a mountain or cross countries
over the nearest golf course, finding

the allure and lost treasure of the natural world.
O my loved one's acreage, her first home
of eternal terrain, her estate that made
Ansel Adams even more famous,

the old neighborhoods are still there, Deer Lodge
still matters to the comfortable
and the desolate. In Cut Bank, people
say, *The cold won't displace us,*

but the wind in Great Falls
continues to blow across Gibson Flats
down to Helena and all the way
to Bozeman, past West Yellowstone

meandering even in our little plain
of southeastern Idaho, finding a way,
still, in the brief hours of summer
to upend and caress the corners of her heart.

Not Quite the River of Tears

I've been the kind to cry the Zambezi
or the Mekong or the Yangtze,
even when I knew it wasn't
my fault. Yes, I've held on
to sentiment long after
it's sailed beyond a league,
swerved from the pathetic to the bathetic
with one too many apologies

and enough syrup to make anyone sick.
And yet I've also hopped
on the buccaneering pendulum,
especially as it's swung
to the other side
where one-word answers
and silence and martyrdom try to tamp down
the sharp edge of what's passive-aggressive,
but in the end words like stones
have shot out of my eyes,
elbows, and mouth.

I yearn to find the spot in between,
that elusive middle ground
where yielding to acknowledgment
opens the door to recognition,
where saying I'm sorry once
and with enough sincerity
prevents any rasp of the new normal
from taking over our lives.

Sacrament

End of January: my future wife
shakes my hand in between
church services. She holds it,
asking for my last name
as if in the answer lies
a brainteaser or crossword puzzle.

I think of saying *Rothstein* or *Greene*,
Mecklenberg or *Gambel*, but all
I can muster is stuttering truth,
a veracious slip of the tongue
that reflects more ego
than id, not some drafty
pick-up line like, "Kiss me if I'm wrong,
but don't I know you?"

Several Januaries later,
it's hard to know whose holding
whose hand in church. We stare
and nod at each other,
absorb the silence of communion,
adjust the children on both sides of us
as trust fixes one palm to the other
like our names spoken together,
like body and bread, vine and leaves.

Liminal Space

Once again, the mountains are beckoning,
                calling you with their silent timbres,

conifer needlework, snowmelt roaring.
                They invite you to traipse, surmise,

and carol like birds at ease or in flight.
                And yes, the deserts, too,—the Mojave

and Sonoran—request an audience
                with your inner child, your Arizonan feet

that once knew the heat of Casa Grande stone.
                Dry, the washes wait for javelina and gila,

for your description of the prickly pear
                and your *rah, rah, rah* like the cactus

wren. But then, there are waterfalls,
                a long fjord, the baptism of a glacial valley:

the 8th wonder, Milford Sound, summoning
                you back to the South Island, to the galactic

views from Mitre and Pembroke Peaks.
                An upwelling shivers in your bones,

loosens your fingers and wrists, begins to taste
                like shepherd's pie, the wind-swept

jargon of rural life and early morning
                ritual of *what to do now?* You are both here

and there, a coming and going between
                spartan necessity and wild places

calling. At your feet is the Welcome mat
                pointing in all directions, you set out

like John Muir with notebook in hand, your mind
                rippling with memory and imagination.

Descent

We have turned onto Highway 7,
descending to Baker City,
to merge with Interstate 84

so our bodies' ache for home
will dissipate. We feel alert
and fiery, our seatbelts newly secured,

as we flap over which book
and stuffed animal belong to whom.
Down through the canyon, trees

arc toward the sun, their light
glimmering in the water
of both leaves and needles.

Ravine to the right. Stony
terrain looms on the left.
A child calls for more breakfast.

Another wants a movie. We shield
our eyes from the thrust
of eastern shine in full luster

now that dawn has scampered.
Galloping through our yearning,
sprinting across the asphalt-top,

a deer bolts out of the rocky
mountainside, hitting the driver's
side of our van, pinwheeling

off the road into the tall, sloping
grass. We're not sure whether to mourn
or pray since we can't turn around

to make an offering. So we do both—
to hope the deer dies quickly
and give thanks for not swerving

across our own lifeline,
all seven of us still trembling
at what it might mean

to witness the dead.

III

Ambrosia

Too often *love* slips
through memory's ring
like blades of grass through a chain link fence.

Or it whimpers
like a dog hobbling back
to his kennel after a fight.

And many times it blows kisses
indiscriminately, even for those waiting
to pawn their junk at the next garage sale.

Too often the hyperbole washes
away a genuine touch
or a soft word after work.

Some days it's commodified,
artificial like light
from a neon sign.

On a few holidays it goes
unexpressed at the right time
but declared in the wrong place.

So sad when it's too little
like a shoebox full of cards
remembered once a year.

But today I saw it,
raw and untutored,
purling and unrushed,

like the river steady
in its waves and offerings,
cutting through the banks

of syrup and restraint,
permanent in high summer sunshine,
constant once the rain has come.

She Calls Me by My First Name

She speaks the monosyllabic word,
the original moniker, as I read a book
in another room. My mind caught

in a drift of story, an author's
wide turn through another country,
when I hear the name

like a footstep in the hall.
I'm not surprised
by the absence of reproof,

neither do I hear the long
wind-up of expectation,
or the requests of mothering.

And I don't wonder
if something is wrong
because "Sweetheart" and "My Love"

have been tucked away,
saved for another occasion.
When she speaks, her voice

patters like early spring rain
and childhood laughter.
Her calling my name

arrives like an unanticipated letter
or a song, I admit,
she teaches me again to sing.

Tree of Life

At dawn she awakens between ground
and scion, her eyes rolling out
of the scabbard darkness, her heart
light as an iris, sharp as a cactus thorn.

The old reflection spins, the worn nimbus
drifts before she forgoes her goods
for a different journey. Her breath
is fig borne out of the scars of lobed leaves,

crafted in the pollen of wasp and silence.
But she refuses silence and vouches
the pome and tang of the newest shoots—
stem, blossom, texture, trench,

thistle and gall rummaging through soil
beside the shaving of rootstock. She crosses
a gulch, scans freezing pockets of field,
climbs to ground with its own slicks of mud.

Up ahead, she's heard of the high spots
hiding muskrats in the bushes
and just beyond, fruit dangles from a cluster
of branches while the light succors a lone,

solitary tree. It gleams like coastline emerging
or the first rapture of rumored snow.
It is more than acacia, more than the hunted
oblation—something between the ark

and its covenant, something outside of mountain
tinder and hillside apex, thousands of axils
entwined in fire, a glow so searing, sprits
and offshoots enflamed and joined together

as others' voices and silhouettes praise incline,
orchard, hedge, residue, taste.
She scales over rocks and stumps
as if they could speak, ignores what she thinks

is mocking, and reaches for the fruit
in its summons and flesh. This beginning
far flung, yet encouraging,
as she basks in color and size, inhales

the juice and aroma between crispness
and candor, this Holy of Holies in scent
and yield, how she sings like the morning wind,
her mouth, a sapphire, with this fiery, luscious bite.

Every Kind of Twin

I've often joked that you and your twin
are as different as Jimmy Carter
and Gerald Ford. Born two minutes apart
in the high New Mexican desert,
straddling midnight between '76 & '77,
two sisters as creative as Abbott & Costello,
as mysterious as Penn & Teller. One who sleeps
and wakes with a book in her hand,
the other who sees the world
like a mechanical engineer. A great
horned owl scouting out the night,
a robin attuned to early morning
weather and songs.

               And although one
knows the contours of urban streets
while the other strolls down
a village lane, maybe
you're more identical than any of us
ever thought, more like skiing partners
who've mastered turns on the local slopes,
unbelieving when the other's amplitude
vaults into the sky. Or perhaps
like golfer and caddy who pace
toward the same bunkers and greens,
forgetting who's who,
eliminating the wrong clubs,
estimating the right angle on a putt.

To be sure, you're backpackers conjoined
in the Grand Canyon of this mortal enterprise—
anticipating switchbacks and vistas—
held together by something as simple
as the way you poach an egg
and as complex as staying the course
on the rough waves of the open sea.

Choice

As July offers its own take
on possibility, the living room
radiating with new furniture,
heat unwinding like ribbon or rope,
21 years after our willingness
to tie the first official knot,
I wonder how our lives
in the curl and loop of decisions
began to intertwine. What hunger
caused you to drop out
of college, buy a Honda Civic,
work for a year (as opposed to two),
land in Missoula instead of Boise
or Bozeman? What propelled me
to delay graduating one semester,
visit shrines in the Holy Land,
drive north, not east,
for the timber of an advanced degree?
Seven false starts, four dead-end
turns, two unwanted semesters
and I would have missed
the singular pitch of your voice,
the silver on a socket wrench,
the aftertaste of pad Thai,
long exhalations of dizziness
on the golf course and ski slope.

What other choices, arbitrary
or blue-printed, microscopic
or colossal, known or unknown,
connected us before we
connected in the evenings
of conversation and awoke
each morning to wide-flung,
Montanan days of bear grass
and breakfast, orchids
and exercise, gentian and sunlight
as simple and sure
as children and phlox?

What I've Thought and What Is

I've wanted to tell people
I saw your name in a phone book—
in the days before cell phones—
called you up to ask for a date
and the rest was history.

I've also wanted to say
we met at the Masters
near Amen Corner
or ran into each other
during the fourth quarter
of the Super Bowl,
but I could never be so glib.

I've thought too about rescue
moments, how I might have saved
you from an abusive relationship
or at least carried you in—
Victorian, British-like—
from a cold rainstorm.

I must say, though, that our story
pushes past any Austen narrative
or renown sporting event. You inhabit
the mind and manners of Elizabeth and Emma
and Eleanor. You are better
than a sideline pick-six
in the last two minutes of a title game.

The phone book had its heyday.
The Super Bowl rules, but only for an afternoon.
As for the English countryside, it is
and always will be
green, yet your beauty, wit,
and warmth transcend that hue
into high desert wonder and revelation—
a knowledge that steadies me
regardless of how gusty or calm the breeze.

44

Remember your 24th birthday,
curling up next to your parents'
wood burning stove, astonished
at the sun's descent at 4:00 p.m.?

Yeah, neither do I.
And yet, we've opened the book
on 20 such commemorations since—
a few times slicing jumble-berry pie,
once staying up till midnight
as if it was an Olympian feat,

and another where we fooled
you into the heat and awe
of a surprise party
ten days late.
                    The details of such
revels drift to homemade omelets,
breakfast in bed, and TV static—
funneled memories and stray thoughts
of flickering candles in Whitefish,
Rexburg, and Palm Desert.

After two decades, your natal day
still opens up like the shine on sterling silver
or the sheen on end-of-year reflections.
It's the never-ending elixir of hot chocolate
only to be eclipsed when we lumber
through January blizzards and shovel
the driveway almost every other day
in the deep maw of winter.

                Today, though,
let's imagine we're pine trees
holding up under heavy snow
and mild December light, steeling ourselves
against sub-zero weather, rising with ageless—
nearly imperceptible—truths,

celebrating the texture and whirl
of one more growth ring
outlining our hair, eyes,
torso, legs—like the swirl
of cake batter and snowflakes,
like the tongue sounding twice
the same numbers,
like the way you pull off
the bow on a perfectly wrapped gift.

Post-Anniversary Thoughts

There is a host of books
to read together and a bathroom mirror
we don't have to look into.

Rain falls like background music
during the credits. Neighborhood dogs
bark only on command.

Spring solstice comes in
and goes out like a lamb.
Owls sound the morning,

drop feathers around noon,
re-appear at night.
Each day after dawn

a nimbus rings
the pine trees. The sun
pulls us from our phones,

out of the van, off the living room
couch. We are frisbees
slowly rising through the air

while our children wave from below.
Our bodies nearly disappear
as the wind carries us about.

Holding Your Hand in Bed

Not so much a grasp or parking spot
but ease and extension—
an under-the-sheets covert
from devices and steering wheels
after the smoky years
of shuttling kids and re-figuring spreadsheets
and weeding in the garden
of pasts and possibilities.
Both of us like baseball gloves
softening in the other's hand.